my itty-bitty bio

Wilma Mankiller

Published in the United States of America by Cherry Lake Publishing Group
Ann Arbor, Michigan
www.cherrylakepublishing.com

Reading Adviser: Beth Walker Gambro, MS, Ed., Reading Consultant, Yorkville, IL
Book Designer: Jennifer Wahl
Illustrator: Jeff Bane

Photo Credits: © RaksyBH/Shutterstock, 5; © ronniejcmc/Shutterstock, 7; © Pressmaster/Shutterstock, 9; © Alex Andrei/Shutterstock, 11; © LR-PHOTO/Shutterstock, 13; © Rena Schild/Shutterstock, 15; © RodClementPhotography /Shutterstock, 17, 22; © Clinton Presidential Library/Image still from White House Television/Wikimedia, 19, 23; © Phil Konstantin/flickr, 21; Jeff Bane, Cover, 1, 6, 8, 18; Various frames throughout, Shutterstock images

Cherry Lake Press is an imprint of Cherry Lake Publishing Group.

Library of Congress Cataloging-in-Publication Data has been filed and is available at catalog.loc.gov

Printed in the United States of America
Corporate Graphics

table of contents

About the author: June Thiele writes and acts in Chicago where they live with their wife and child. June is Dena'ina Athabascan and Yup'ik, Indigenous cultures of Alaska. They try to get back home to Alaska as much as possible.

About the illustrator: Jeff Bane and his two business partners own a studio along the American River in Folsom, California, home of the 1849 Gold Rush. When Jeff's not sketching or illustrating for clients, he's either swimming or kayaking in the river to relax.

my story

I was born in 1945. I grew up in a big **Cherokee** family. I had 10 **siblings**. We lived in Oklahoma.

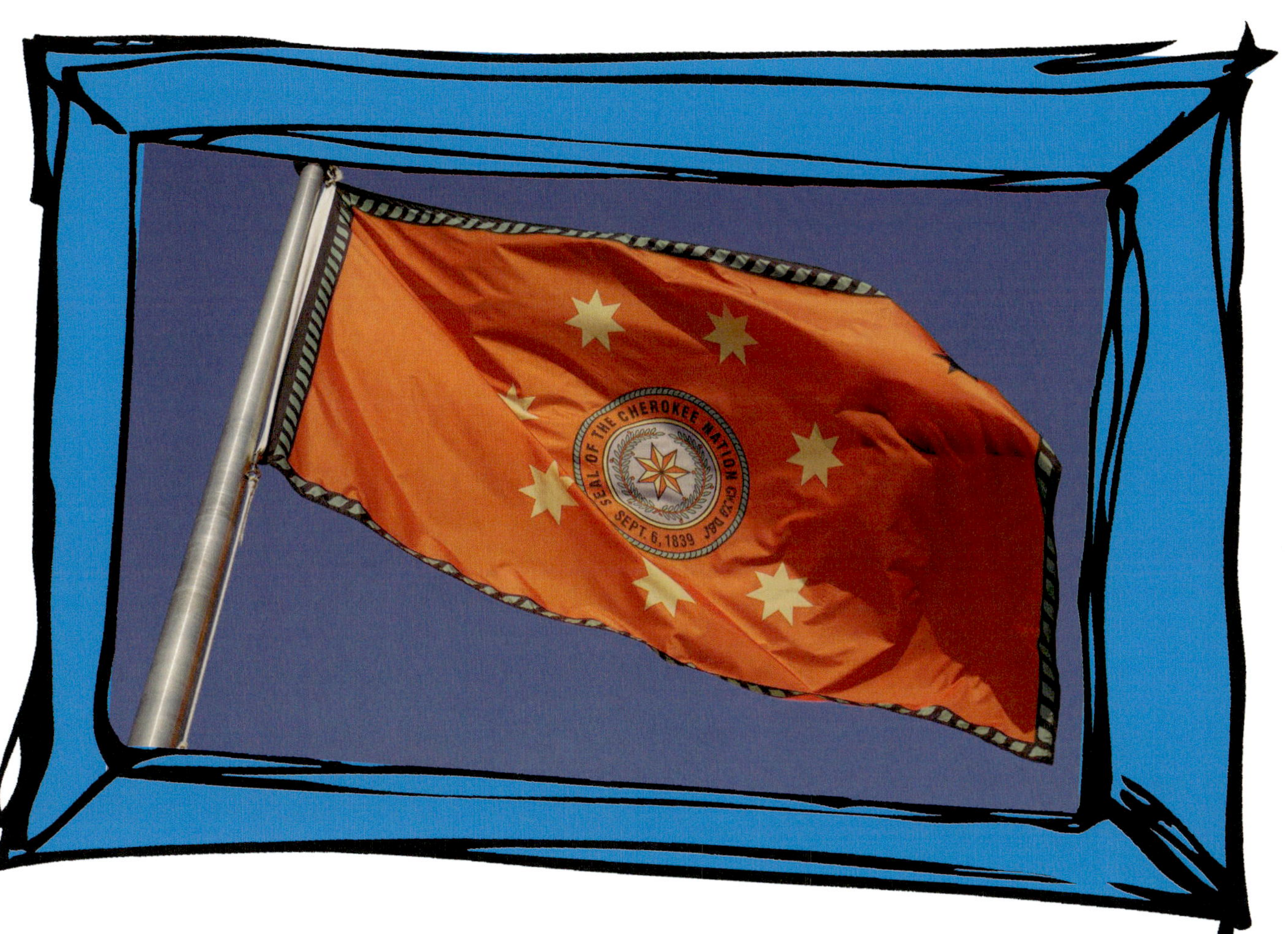
SEAL OF THE CHEROKEE NATION
SEPT. 6, 1839

I grew up in a tiny house. We didn't have a lot of money. There wasn't even electricity! But we made do. We had a garden. We fished. My mom sewed.

What's your family like?

We moved to California. But I struggled. I didn't like school. Kids made fun of me. I was happy when I graduated from high school.

I fell in love. I got married and had two daughters. I also went to college.

Then the **Occupation** of Alcatraz happened. This was a **protest** led by **Indigenous** people. I was inspired. I became an **activist**.

INDIANS
WELCOME
UNITED STATES
PENITENTIARY
ALCATRAZ ISLAND AREA 12 ACRES
1½ MILES TO TRANSPORT DOCK
ONLY GOVERNMENT BOATS PERMITTED
OTHERS MUST KEEP OFF 200 YARDS
NO ONE ALLOWED ASHORE
WITHOUT A PASS

I helped make lasting changes for my people. I created organizations. I wrote books. I gave talks. I made my people strong. I improved their jobs, education, and health.

I AM
ON
INDIGENOUS
LAND
U R
ON
INDIGENOUS
LAND
WE R
ON
INDIGENOUS
LAND

I became the **chief** of the Cherokee Nation. I was the first woman to do this!

WELCOME
TO THE
CHEROKEE INDIAN
RESERVATION

I received many honors and awards. They included the **Presidential Medal of Freedom**.

What are you proud of?

I died in 2010. But I continue to inspire others. Many Indigenous leaders look to my life for direction.

What would you like to ask me?

timeline

1985

1940

Born
1945

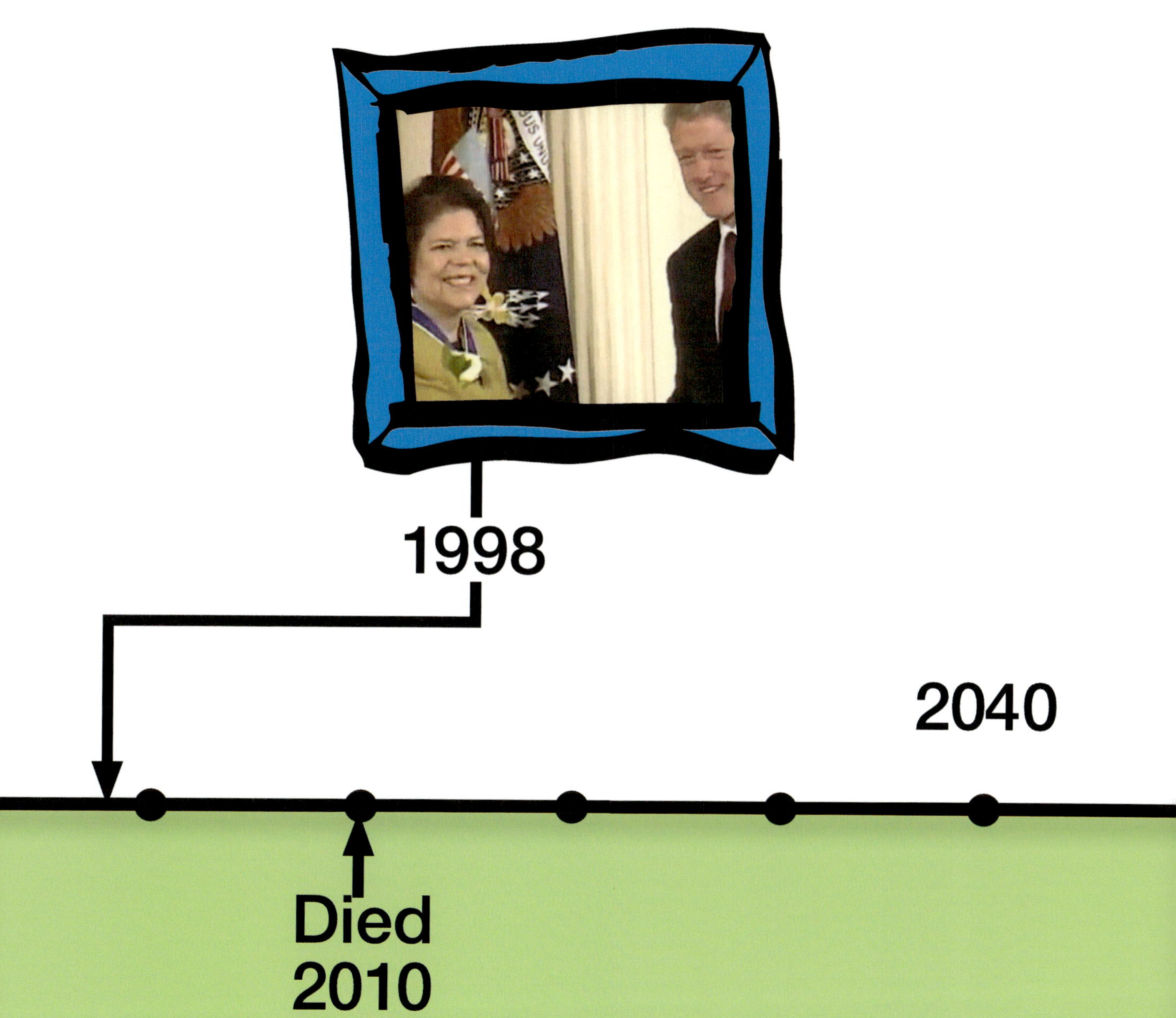
1998
2040
Died
2010

glossary

activist (AK-tih-vist) a person who brings about change

Cherokee (CHAYR-uh-kee) a group of Indigenous people who live in much of Oklahoma

chief (CHEEF) a person in a leading position

Indigenous (in-DIH-juh-nuhss) born or occurring naturally in a particular place; native

occupation (ah-kyuh-PAY-shuhn) the activity of taking control of a place

Presidential Medal of Freedom (preh-zuh-DEN-shuhl MEH-duhl UHV FREE-duhm) the highest civilian honor a person in the United States can receive

protest (PROH-test) an event where people gather to show strong disapproval about something

siblings (SIH-blings) brothers and sisters

index